PRISCILLA'S HOMECOMING ACROSS THE SEA

By Stacey Culpepper
Illustrations by Thinh Nguyen

ISBN-13 978-0996138437

©Stacey Ann Culpepper 2015

This is a true story that follows the life of a young girl re-named Priscilla who was torn away from her village in Sierra Leone and sold into slavery. Young readers will be inspired to learn that out of bad experiences persistent courage can lead to triumph.

This book is dedicated to my husband Charles, Mom, Dad, April, Robee and Maurice.

Stacey Culpepper has been writing since the age of seven. She decided to make her works public because she saw a great need for diversity in YA literature and storytellers. Living in diverse environments stimulated her already active imagination at a young age and enhanced her zest for multiculturalism. Stacey believes young readers need to see themselves in positive writings in order to thrive. Her goal is to make diverse stories easily accessible to young people everywhere.

Thinh Nguyen is an artist who grew up in Southern California where his shyness helped to hone his natural ability to draw. He chose to pursue a career in art, with the loving support of his family. He holds a BFA from the Rocky Mountain College of Art + Design where he studied animation. Drawings that exhibit personality and narrative are the most interesting to him, and he strives to inject those qualities into his artwork. Thinh currently resides in Arizona.

PRISCILLA'S HOMECOMING ACROSS THE SEA

No one knows her real name. During the hot summer months, she could have possibly spent time braiding a friend's hair into neat twisted cornrows under a shady tropical drumstick tree. She probably went to town regularly to sell baskets and cloths made by her mother and the other women of her village.

She also could have spent many summer afternoons running through plush, green rainforests in the countryside. We know that she was part of the Mende (men-dee) people who were farmers in rice-growing communities. But in 1756, slave traders raided her village and kidnapped her.

The name of her country is called Sierra Leone, which means 'Lion Mountain' in the Portuguese language. It is pronounced (see-air-uh lee-ohn) and is a country the size of the state of Illinois. It is located on the west coast of Africa between the modern day countries of the Republic of Guinea and Liberia. It is usually hot and humid in the summer, but rains a lot between the months of April and September.

The Portuguese explored the country in the 15th century and the British later made it a colony.

The little girl might have been asleep one morning beneath a grass roof on a bed made of clay. She probably did not even have a chance to run away but was quickly taken and then shackled with other women who were then forced to march barefoot through the countryside towards the Atlantic Ocean.

No doubt she was tired, hungry, sad, and extremely afraid. The little girl finally made it to Bunce Island, which was a British slave castle on the coast of Sierra Leone. This was a noisy trading post where Africans were bought, imprisoned, and loaded aboard ships that took them on middle passages to the Americas.

We know this little girl was put on a ship named the *Hare*, which had come from Newport, Rhode Island in the United States. The captain of the ship, Caleb Godfrey, kept meticulous records on his ship's log. He noted the voyage back to the United States from Africa began on April 9, 1756 and he had 84 slaves on board, including four little boys and two little girls.

The voyage took two and a half months to reach the United States. Sixteen people died on the trip to Charleston, South Carolina. There was sickness, confusion, and darkness on these ships.

The little girl probably did not know what a ship was or where she was going. She could not even understand what the captain's crew was saying to her.

Upon reaching land, the little girl and four other children were bought on June 30, 1756 by a rice grower named Elias Ball Jr. for about $900 dollars.

Mr. Ball gave all the children English names and called the little girl Priscilla. He did not know her exact age, but marked her in his records as being 10-years-old.

The newly named 10-year-old Priscilla was taken to the Ball's Comingtee Plantation where she lived for the rest of her life. She would be forever separated from her family, friends, and home back in her village nestled in the greenery of Sierra Leone.

Plantation records show that Priscilla eventually married a man named Jeffrey and they had 10 children and 30 grandchildren.

Priscilla must have been a strong and courageous little girl because she grew up to become the ancestress to about 75,000 African Americans in the United States today.

Edward Ball was a descendant of Elias Ball. In 1998 he wrote a book called, _Slaves in the Family_ where he used his family's slave records and other sources to research the lives of former slaves like Priscilla and trace her family tree.

Edward wanted to understand his family's past dealings with slaves and share with those slaves' descendants a piece of their history.

He found that Priscilla died in 1811 and was buried on the plantation, near the Cooper River. Her grave cannot be found, but a record of her life- her kidnapping, children, and legacy all survived in the Ball's family slave lists, ledgers, and receipts. This is very unusual because there are very few detailed paper trails left from this time period.

	29	M	F
Bruno	20	M	B
William	17	F	B
Virgina	12	M	B
Walter	10	F	B
Prisilla	7	F	B
Rachel .			

Tomalind Martin Polite is one of Priscilla's descendants. She is her great, great, great, great, great, great, granddaughter and teaches children in South Carolina speech therapy. Edward Ball helped Tomalind to discover Priscilla's beginning.

The government of Sierra Leone invited Tomalind to come back to Africa and meet the rest of Priscilla's African family, in May 2005.

They did not speak the same language, or have the same culture but all shared the story of a little girl lost who was later found through records.

Priscilla would have been proud of her descendant Tomalind who was openly welcomed to a strange land in her behalf.

In 1756, a 10-year-old African girl was kidnapped. She was transported to South Carolina, renamed Priscilla, and then sold into slavery.

Because of the discovery of a 252 year old paper trail, Priscilla could at last be embraced as the long lost daughter from across the sea, who had finally found her way back home.

Please read more about Stacey and her other diverse children's book on her website @www.staceyculpepper.com

Diverse Culpepper Books

ISBN-13 978-0996138437

ISBN-10 0996138439

Bibliography for "Homecoming"

Book

Ball, Edward. *Slaves In The Family.* New York: Farrar, Straus, and Giroux, 1998.

Web Sites

The University of South Florida and the African Heritage Project, 2008 http://www.yale.edu/glc/priscilla/bib.htm. Accessed 05/15/08.

http://www.Center for the Study of Slavery, Resistance, and Abolition in collaboration with Joseph Opala.

http://www.africanaheritage.com/PriscillasHomecoming.asp. Maintained by Gilder Lehrman. Accessed 05/30/08.